Bringing
Home
The
Prodigals

Bringing Home The Prodigals

Rob Parsons

Authentic

COLORADO SPRINGS · MILTON KEYNES · HYDERABAD

Authentic Publishing
We welcome your questions and comments.

USA   1820 Jet Stream Drive, Colorado Springs, CO 80921   www.authenticbooks.com
UK   9 Holdom Avenue, Bletchley, Milton Keynes, Bucks, MK1 1QR
         www.authenticmedia.co.uk
India   Logos Bhavan, Medchal Road, Jeedimetla Village, Secunderabad 500 055, A.P.

Bringing Home The Prodigals
ISBN-13: 978-1-934068-69-4
ISBN-10: 1-934068-69-1

10 09   / 6 5 4 3

Published in 2008 by Authentic

Cover design: projectluz.com
Interior design: projectluz.com
Editorial team: KJ Larson, Tom Richards

Printed in the United States of America

Contents

Dedication

To Sheron Rice, who has worked alongside me for over twelve years, with more thanks than I can possibly say. You are one of God's gifts to me.

And to my friend Rhys Williams. May you fulfill your dreams. Keep the faith.

Acknowledgements

Many people have helped with *Bringing Home the Prodigals* but special thanks to Jonathan Booth, Sheron Rice, Steve Williams, Andrew Cooper, Kate Hancock, and the people at Prayer for Revival who began it all. Thanks also to Keith Danby, Volney James, Kay Larson and the whole team at Authentic, and to my agents, Eddie Bell and Pat Lomax of the Bell Lomax Agency.

Thank you also to those who contributed prayers and reflections, especially Wendy Bray, who bore the lion's share of that.

We gratefully acknowledge permission to use the following poems:

The poem on page 42 is taken from *When Life Takes What Matters* by Susan Lenzkes, copyright ©1993. Used by permission of Discovery House Publishers, Box 3566, Grand Rapids, Michigan 49501. All rights reserved.

The poem on page 54 is taken from *Prodigals and Those Who Love Them* by Ruth Bell Graham, copyright © 1991. Used by permission of Focus on the Family Publishing, Colorado Springs, CO 80935 3550. All rights reserved.

And finally, thank you to those who allowed their stories to be told.

CHAPTER ONE

Always Leave a Light On

Sometimes God ambushes us: it happened to me on March 14, 1998. I had been invited to speak at the National Exhibition Center in the UK to thousands of people who had gathered to pray for the return of their prodigals. I had prepared a message based on the timeless parable of the lost son, and it was folded securely in the inside pocket of my jacket. I believed I was ready to deliver God's word.

I have been at many Christian events over the years, but I have never experienced the wave of emotion that filled the

> Sometimes God ambushes us.

auditorium that day. The organizers had seated my wife, Dianne, and me on the platform, and as I gazed out at that vast audience, I couldn't help but wonder what stories lay behind the prayers.

Somewhere, no doubt, was a woman whose husband had once led a church and been a faithful husband and father until the night he told her the four things that so many Christian men tell their wives when they leave them for another woman: "We were so young when we got married we hardly knew what we were doing—I doubt we ever really loved each other"; "In the long run this will be better for you"; "One day you'll realize this is best for the kids," and "I've prayed about this, and it's OK with God."

And somewhere there was a father who had told his tiny daughter Bible stories. She had picked one each night from the huge children's Bible they kept on the shelf in her bedroom. They had said prayers together, and he had always been touched that, from her youngest days, she had prayed for others more than herself. But as he prayed in the auditorium that day, he thought of her later teenage years and the gradual disinterest in anything to do with God. A great sobbing convulsed his body as he remembered the night he found the drugs in her bedroom and, finally, the day she left, cursing both him and God.

These people had gathered, every one of them with a prodigal on their hearts: friends, brothers, husbands, wives, and sometimes in a strange reversal of the parable, mothers and fathers—but mostly children.

Every one of them with a prodigal on their hearts...

But that great arena did not hold only people praying. In the very front was a huge wooden cross. Its shadow seemed to reach over the whole crowd. During the day, people were invited to write the name of their prodigal on a small card, bring it to the front, and lay it at the foot of the cross. I watched them as they came: young people bringing the names of school friends, married couples holding hands as they laid down the names of children, friends walking together clutching cards, and often the elderly, shuffling forward and bending slowly as they lay the names of those they loved at the cross.

After an hour or so one of the organizers asked me if I would leave the platform and stand by the cross to pray with some of those who were coming forward. Of course I agreed and made my way to the floor of the arena and to the cross. That's when God ambushed me. What occurred in the next two minutes changed my life forever and was the impetus that was to take the message of "Bringing Home the Prodigals" around the world.

When I reached the cross there were tens of thousands of names there. They were written on cards that were spilling off the little table at the foot of the cross and onto the floor. I picked up and read some of them: "Jack" "Milly" "Bring Charles home, Lord." It seemed to me that the pain of the world lay at the foot of that cross. I thank God for what he has done in the lives of our two children, but at that time Dianne and I had heavy hearts for them, and I remember laying Katie's name at the foot of the cross and Lloyd's name next to hers. And then I started to cry. I could not stop.

There were tens of thousands of names there.

As I wept, God laid a message about prodigals on my heart that I first preached later that day. It was not the neat, nicely wrapped-up one with all the answers—that was in my pocket. It was a message forged from brokenness and a sense of utter dependence on God. As I finished speaking that day, I remember thinking that one day I would put it into a book.

But life for all of us is busy and the book was never started. And then one day, as part of some routine tests, the doctors found a possible abnormality with one of my kidneys. They feared it was tumor. I had about ten days to wait for the results of the tests that would determine what the problem was.

On one of those days I found myself ambling along a London street. It was a wonderful spring morning; on such days, London is at its best. The air was crisp, the sky blue, and behind me the sun shone off Westminster Abbey and St. Margaret's Chapel as I made my way past Churchill's War Rooms and into St. James' Park.

The park was almost deserted, and the pigeons, squirrels, and I looked at each other as if there was little else of interest. Never does life become as precious as when you think it may be suddenly shortened. I began to think about things that really mattered to me. The message of the prodigals came to my mind, and I knew I had to get that book written. I started it that week. A few days later the test results came and were favorable: I did not have a tumor—just an over-sized kidney that I'd probably had all my life. A few months later the book was written. But that was only the beginning.

One day the people who had invited me to preach at their day of prayer in the National Exhibition Center in Birmingham in the UK called to ask me to meet with them. They said God had told them to pass on to me the mantle of the burden for prodigals that they had carried for so many years. We began to visit the denominational leaders to see if the message resonated with them. Without exception—whether it was the Salvation Army, the Baptists, Catholics, Methodists, or even the Archbishop of Canterbury himself—the response was the same: "This is a God-given word for today. We support you in it."

Over the following few years in auditoriums all across the United Kingdom, more than fifty thousand people have experienced a Bringing Home the Prodigals event. Even now in my mind's eye, I can picture them listening to the message and bringing the names of their prodigals to the foot of the cross. We began to hear the most remarkable stories of prodigals coming back to God.

Since then we have been taking Bringing Home the Prodigals all over the world. I have watched people stream forward to lay the names of their prodigals at the cross in Costa Rica, Uganda, South Africa, Malaysia, Singapore, Borneo, Australia, New Zealand, Ireland, and North America. This little book contains the heart of the message of Bringing Home the Prodigals I believe God has laid on my heart. I warn you now; it is a simple message. Most of us feel we know the parable so well that there is hardly anything new we could learn. Maybe this is true, but God wants to remind us of what we knew in our hearts all along—and somehow forgot.

It is a simple message.

I wrote part of the book in a small conference center on the Gower coast near Swansea, Wales. It is not far from where Dylan Thomas wrote "Under Milk Wood." The building is set on a hill, and the view from my window was unspeakably beautiful, running across fields, then woods, and finally ending at the sea in the great sweep of the Bay. One morning I took a break from writing and stood outside the house gazing into the distance at the breakers hitting the beach. After a few minutes I was joined by a priest. He had on the traditional long black cassock, had a flowing grey beard, and wore what my kids used to call "Jesus sandals." He had been leading a discussion in one of the seminar rooms and said he had "just come out to get a little air whilst they ponder a couple of theological teasers I've set them."

He told me a most moving story.

We began chatting and he asked me what I was doing. When I told him I was writing a book about prodigals, he told me a most moving story. Let me try to capture his words as I remember them:

In a village near here, is a large old house. An elderly lady lives there alone and every night, as darkness falls, she puts a light on in the attic. Her son left home twenty-five years ago, rather like the prodigal in the parable, but she has never given up the hope that one day he will come home. We all know the house well, and although the bulb must occasionally need replacing, none of us have ever seen that house without a light on. It is for her son.

None of us have ever seen that house without a light on.

The theme of "leaving a light on" has become a recurring one in the letters and emails I have received from all over the world from those who wait for a prodigal's return. Shortly after one of the Bringing Home the Prodigals events, a woman wrote to me. She told me that her daughter had walked out of their home when she was eighteen years old. She had turned her back not only on her mother and father, but on the God she had once loved. "My daughter didn't get in touch, and we didn't know whether she was alive or dead" the woman wrote. She went on to tell me that every night, as she and her husband turned off the lights before they went to bed, she would always say to him, "Leave the porch light on." And every Christmas, she would put a little Christmas tree in the front of the house, its lights shining, just as she used to when her daughter was at home.

After six years, her daughter suddenly came home—and not just to her mother and father, but to God. When she did, she told her mother a remarkable story: "Mom, I so often wanted to come home, but I was too ashamed. Sometimes, in the early hours of the morning, I would drive my car into your street and just sit there. I used to gaze at the houses and every one of them was dark apart from our house: you always left a light on. And at Christmas I would do the same: just sit there in the darkness and look at the Christmas tree you had put outside—I knew it was for me."

I have never been able to get that mother out of my mind. She seems to me to symbolize the hopes, fears, and prayers of millions across the world whose hearts are breaking for their prodigals. But this is not just a message for them; in fact *Bringing Home the Prodigals* is not just about praying for our prodigals to come home. It is about asking us to consider the characters of our local churches. Is it possible that by our attitudes, our concern with rules and regulations that are not on God's heart, or by our ingrained spirit of the elder brother (or sister!) we have made it easy for some to leave? Perhaps we have kept them out of mind while they are gone and tragically made it harder for them to return. Could it be that inadvertently we have "created" prodigals?

This is a theme that should catch the imagination of all who care about evangelism. The truth is, most of us know ten people who may have never been to church whom we'd like to invite to an evangelistic service—but we all know a *hundred* prodigals. The numbers are enormous. When the prodigals come home we are going to have to pull down our old church buildings and use aircraft hangers. If you care about church growth, then care about this message. There is nothing as frustrating as seeing people come to Christ through the front door of the church and losing others in almost the same proportion out the door at the back.

> Have we made it easy for some to leave?

All over the world I have cried with parents for their prodigals. There is no more fervent prayer in homes today than, "Father, bring our prodigal home." I have concentrated in this book on those who have children, of whatever age, who are prodigals, but of course there are many kinds of prodigals—brothers, sisters, husbands, wives, and friends. I hope with all my heart that for whomever you are concerned, you will find something here to encourage you and keep the flames of hope alight.

There are many kinds of prodigals.

This book is not written principally to give advice, although I will share with you the lessons I have learned from many whose hearts have cried out to God for those they love. My hope is that it will be a book that will release us from false guilt, bring us hope, and above all, lead us to prayer. At the end of every chapter is a prayer and reflection; each one is written by someone who has cried for a prodigal and who has come to believe that, ultimately, God is our only hope. At the very end of the book we will each bring our prodigals to the cross of Christ.

Pray that we will catch the Father's heart for the prodigals.

And we should not pray just for our prodigals, but for ourselves as well. We can pray that we will catch the Father's heart for the prodigals—the outrageous grace of the One who, even as we stumble down the long road home, runs to throw a robe on our back, put a ring on our finger and shoes on our feet. And if we do change, if we can catch something of that father-heart of God, then it may be that, in his great mercy, he will touch the lives of thousands of our prodigals—and bring them home.

Love from the Father

When the night fell
When the stars shone
When the thin clouds dusted
When the air was cold
When the world was quiet
I sat on the grass and thought
About who I was and what I did.
And I was scared.
I thought about how I was wrong
How carelessly I hurt people
How I was cruel to those I love.
I looked at the stars searchingly
And I found myself asking God to forgive me.
I sat in silence listening to everything
But hearing nothing.
Then God touched me, lifted me.
I walked home and found a note,
A message on my door.
I forgive you my child, love from the father.

A seventeen-year-old boy
(This was his first poem)

Chapter Two

Who are the Prodigals?

It is true that the parable of the prodigal son is two thousand years old, but it is being re-enacted every day in homes all across our world as thousands of mothers and fathers wait up until the early hours of the morning for their children to come home. It is being re-lived in the homes where in the children's bedrooms the drugs were first found, being played out again in the tears, the pain and the sheer frustration of the broken dreams and the crying out of, "Where did we go wrong?"

This is a modern story. Perhaps it is *our* story for, of a certainty, there is no family, no matter how godly, how expert at parenting, or how devoted to each other, who is immune from the circumstances that cause us to cry out to God for our children.

This simple parable has been called the greatest short story in

> This simple parable has been called the greatest short story in the world.

the world. It is the tale of the boy who broke his father's heart and yet could not destroy the love the father had for him. We find it difficult in our modern culture to take in the full impact of what this young man did. He was not just seeking to sow a few wild oats; he was turning his back on everything his father, his community, and his very upbringing had taught him. He would not, in the time-honored way of Eastern communities, wait for his father to die before he received his inheritance. He wanted it all now. In essence he was saying, "I wish you were dead already."

The money ran out, the friends left, and he was destitute.

The boy took his money and went to what Dr. Luke calls "a distant country"— as far as he could possibly get from his father, from the influences and the things that restricted him at home. In fact he got so far from his Jewish roots that he was in a place where they kept pigs. He had more money than he ever dreamt of and more friends than he ever hoped for, and whatever we want to make of it, this boy was having fun. He was partying as if it was going out of style, and you get the feeling that he wished he'd left the old man's house earlier. Then it happened: the money ran out, the friends left, and he was destitute—not just economically, but socially and spiritually. He was in the pits—and he was alone.

Apart from death, there was nowhere else for this young man to go.

It would have been hard for Jesus to have painted a more graphic illustration for a Jewish audience of how low this boy had sunk than for him to have told them that the boy found himself in a pig-sty, debating whether or not to eat the animals' food. Those who listened that day understood the message well: apart from death, there was nowhere else for this young man to go.

But as the boy sat in that sty something happened. If the money had not run out, or if the famine had not come, it might not have occurred, but one day "he came to his senses." And the second he did, his mind went back to home. It was the tragedy of his situation that eventually cleared his mind; it was the hunger that made him consider going home, and it was the shame that made him decide on the speech. He would go to his father and say, "I have sinned against heaven and against you." As he put the words together, some of those sins came flooding back to him and he added, "I am no longer worthy to be called your son. Make me like one of the hired servants." He reasoned that if he came back as a servant then at least his father could kick him out if he wanted to—the hired help could be dismissed at a day's notice; they had even less status than the slaves. And so he began the long walk home.

And that is how it would have ended—with a boy coming back full of shame, eating humble pie, and a father saying, "I told you so. Why didn't you listen to your mother and me?" Or even worse, it could have ended like it did for a prodigal I heard about in Australia. After many years away, the boy eventually decided to come home. The track to the farm where his parents lived was over a mile long. He trudged up it in trepidation, rehearsing what he would say. As he passed the final bend in the road, he saw the lights of the house. His spirits began to lift, and finally he was at the front porch. He knocked on the door. His father opened it and gazed at him.

"Dad, I'm home."

His father said, "I have no son" and closed the door. They never saw each other again.

The story of the prodigal son *could* have ended just like that—except that this father had never given up on his son. He had never stopped looking down the road, and he had never stopped loving.

> This father had never given up on his son.

Because the father had never given up hope, before the boy saw him, he saw the boy. And he began to run. As he reached his son, he threw his arms around him and began kissing him. The young man tried to begin his speech but never did manage to finish it—never did get to the part that said, "Make me your servant"—because the old man was shouting to the servants: "Quick! Put a robe on his back, a ring on his finger, and shoes on his feet! Start preparing a party! My boy's home!"

The making of a prodigal

It is without doubt a wonderful story, and the important question for us is: "Who are the prodigals today?" The truth is we have made prodigals of some who never were prodigals in the first place.

> We have made prodigals of some who never were prodigals in the first place.

My parents didn't go to church but they sent me to the chapel on the corner of our street. I remember Miss Williams, the Sunday School teacher, coming to call for me when I was four years old. Those good people in that little church changed my life. But sometimes even they got it wrong.

I was nineteen years old. My friends Jim and Sally were a little older than me and engaged to be married. With about six months to go to until the wedding, Sally became pregnant. The news traveled around the youth group pretty fast, and of course, it soon reached the elders too. On Sunday morning, at the end of the service, one of the elders stood in the pulpit and told us all that because of the shame this young couple had brought on the church they could no longer be part of our little fellowship. It's true that he read some Scriptures he said proved the elders' decision was right, but even though I knew I was no theologian, I sensed a terrible wrong was being done. I remember saying to him, "You're a shepherd of the sheep. You're meant to care for them when they get into trouble, not kick them out of the flock when they've got a broken leg."

We didn't see Jim and Sally again in church for almost thirty-five years and then, one Sunday morning, in they came. They were grey haired now; they had been faithful to each other all those years and had brought up their little girl to be a fine young woman. I am sure in those intervening thirty-five years many people viewed them as prodigals, but somehow I doubt they ever turned their back on either God or the church. No, I think maybe we *made* them prodigals.

But we don't create prodigals over just the big issues, such as the one faced by my young friends. We have made people prodigals because of the color of their hair or because they had various body piercings or tattoos. A woman told me that when she was in her early twenties an older woman in her church had said to her, "My dear, godly women don't wear Doc Martin boots." Of course we smile, but in reality it is a tragedy. A vicar's wife told me of an incident in her church. Her sixteen-year-old son had stopped attending church, but one Easter Sunday he told his parents he'd like

> We don't create prodigals over just the big issues.

to come to the service. Well, as you can imagine, these parents were thrilled, but there was a problem: their son had taken to wearing a baseball cap everywhere, and they were afraid he would wear it to church. He did. As the family sat there together, they could feel the stares at the backs of their heads and hear the whispers that said, "Why does that young man have a hat on in church?" and "Why does the *vicar's son* have a hat on in church?" I quite understand it was probably better that he didn't have a hat on in church, but I doubt heaven was having committee meetings about it.

The truth is that many of us carry a little bag on our backs. It is labeled "How to Be a Good Christian." The bag contains, among other things, the way we have been taught to worship, to tithe, our attitude toward alcohol, the way we use our money, the movies we watch, the way we think we hear God's voice, and our attitude about politics.

> Many of us carry a bag on our backs labeled "How to Be a Good Christian."

In my more foolish moments I kid myself that I have managed to lose the bag—that I am now free of it—but the truth is the old bag will not so easily be laid down. Each of us is tied more closely to our culture than we can possibly imagine. The great danger, both to myself and others, is when I decide to put my bag on the shoulders of another Christian. Jesus caught the religious leaders of his time doing this and he hated it: "You lay burdens on their shoulders that they just can't bear." The dreadful implication was that God looked at things differently from them, and that maybe the bags they carried were filled with all the wrong stuff anyway.

Everywhere I go I meet prodigals who tried hard to carry the "How to Be a Good Christian" bags that others put on their backs, but eventually the bags became too heavy for them and they laid them down. In so doing, they believed they'd disappointed God, and so they left the church. I ask them what was in the bag they carried—what it was people had told them mattered to God. Sometimes their answers make me cry.

A mother wrote to me:

> *Vicky has never been a conformer. In church she didn't want to sew banners: she wanted to play football with the boys. She ran away when she was fifteen and from that point decided she didn't want to go to church anymore. This happened not long after she had helped to give out coffees following a service and had accidentally spilled some down a leader's shirt. She was rebuked. I saw the hurt in her eyes. Here was a bumbling teenager trying to win approval and failing.*
>
> *I suppose we didn't help. She always wanted to wear jeans, but we taught her the leadership line that "Girls should wear dresses to church." Instead of being that creative, awesome, radical young person who demonstrated her love of God differently from others, she was judged and knocked down. Vicky is in her twenties now, and we have a good relationship. I will never give up praying for her return to faith.*
>
> *Perhaps one day I'll write a book, called, "Why little girls don't have to wear dresses in church."*

Eventually the bag becomes too heavy.

Lord, help me to truly know what matters to you.

It seems to me that one of our most urgent prayers should be, "Lord, help me to truly know what matters to you and, if necessary, lay down my life for it. But help me also to recognize what is just my particular bag."

It is a great tragedy that in the modern church so often we judge each other by rules and regulation we have devised ourselves, which have nothing to do with following Christ. So often, it is with this un-written code that we "create" our prodigals. In various Christian cultures across the world a person can be written off as a prodigal over something that in another culture is accepted. My friend Dr. R.T. Kendall (who is American) summed it up for me. He told me that when a group of German Christians saw some American Christians with all their gold and diamonds on, they were so shocked they dropped their cigars in their beer.

I remember an older man telling us that when he was a boy he used to help his father give out tracts entitled "Should Baptists dance?" There is many a church leader who has been approached by a representative of the deaconate or the elder board saying, "Pastor, we say this in love, but some of us are very worried about the behavior of your children. We've noticed that one of them has body piercing/dresses all in black/started smoking/goes to nightclubs."

And so it begins—the making of a prodigal.

There is nothing new in this. In every age there have been those who are more concerned with religion than faith and who are quick to point out where somebody has missed *their* particular mark. The Pharisees came to Jesus and said, "Why do your dis-

> In the eyes of the religious leaders of his time, Jesus himself was a prodigal.

ciples eat with unwashed hands?" and "Why don't your disciples fast?" They were saying, "Your own people are going off the road, what are you going to do about it?"

In the eyes of the religious leaders of his time, Jesus himself was a prodigal. They noted that he ate with sinners. Time and time again they reminded him of their own adherence to the rules and regulations that, in their eyes, meant they were right with God, but this didn't stop Jesus living his life outside of the protection of the religious ghetto. It's easy for some Christians to see others as prodigals because they themselves live in such an unreal world. Some of our young people who are written off as prodigals are trying to follow Christ in a world that exists outside of the Christian goldfish bowl. In contrast, many Christians not only don't have one friend who doesn't share their Christian faith—they don't have one friend who doesn't share their *particular brand* of the Christian faith. The great challenge to the church is that Jesus' love and acceptance of those the religious leaders viewed as beyond the pale did not involve him in compromise. The incredible thing is not that Jesus ate with sinners—you'd expect the one who came to save the lost to do that. No, the incredible thing is that sinners *ate with Jesus.* He was the Holy One—the one without a *hint* of compromise—and yet sinners wanted to be near him. I think it's fair to say that often "sinners" don't want to be near us, but it's not because we are holy—it's because we don't really know what it is to be holy; we can't understand what it is to love.

I have observed a strange thing about those we call "prodigals": they sometimes have a keener sense of their sin than those who stay in the church. I can remember sitting in on annual general church meetings and listening as the members slandered one another, gossiped about each another over coffee, and then conspired to drive the pastor crazy with the bitterest of criticism. It seems sometimes that we who stay in church grow a little more comfortable with our sin than some of those who have left it.

Who are the prodigals anyway?

Who are the prodigals anyway? Consider this: a man has two sons. Both seem to be followers of Christ although the younger one, Jack, has always been something of a rebel. It was Jack who slipped a goldfish into the baptistery, and yes, it was he who, when he was twelve, put vodka into the speaker's water jar on the pulpit. Stephen, on the other hand, seemed a model child, and in later life—and true to form—he never rocked the boat very much.

When he was twenty years old, Jack stopped going to church. He found it so hard to fit in and often felt more of a sense of fellowship in the pub than he ever did in the prayer meeting. Eventually he left home and moved to a big city.

He immediately started to work with homeless people. It was hard work. He was often conned out of the little money he earned, was beaten up twice, and was once arrested for standing up for a woman who slept in a shop doorway and was about to have her few possessions put into a dumpster outside an Oxford Street store. Jack had a wonderful heart for people. Sometimes their pain would make him cry.

The other son, Stephen, never stopped going to church. In fact Stephen rarely missed any meeting at all, and it wasn't long before he was asked to join the deaconate. Here he proved to be efficient and dedicated—and a complete pain. He spoke rudely to people, was ungracious, and made the pastor's life an absolute misery. Stephen had strong opinions on how things should be done and often said, "It's important to have high standards for the sake of the church." People frequently found it hard to meet those standards—whether it was the worship leader, the youth pastor, or the single-parent mother whose kids would sometimes disturb the family service—and when they failed, Stephen told them so.

Which of those two sons was a prodigal? The answer is both. And both needed to come home.

Before we go any further, it is absolutely vital that we define what "coming home" means. I believe that church attendance is important—almost every Sunday of my life I am in my own church—but church attendance is not the only way to decide whether someone is a prodigal or not. In Christian circles if somebody asks us how our kids are doing spiritually, as long as they attend church on Sunday and one mid-week meeting that seems to gives us the right to say, "I'm pleased to say they are following Christ." But do they *love* Christ? Do they care for the poor? Do they stand up for injustice when they see it? Can they forgive, or do they harbor grudges? Are they compassionate? Patient? And is there any evidence that slowly they are becoming a little more like the one they follow?

We desperately need God's wisdom in dealing with this. We dare not get it wrong, for if we do, we not only allow some in deep spiritual need to remain in our complacency, but we also drive away those who never did turn their back on God at all. I fear there are many children who hear regularly from their parents that they are praying for them to return to God but who really need to hear their encouragement for the things they are doing that please God.

> Which of those two sons was a prodigal? The answer is both.

The great problem with the church in the Western world is that half the prodigals are still in the pews.

The great problem with the church in the Western world is that half the prodigals are still in the pews. It's true that our wrongs may not be as easy to see as those of others, but in our hearts we know that we are as far away: the boy in the parable wasted his life in riotous living—we are eaten away with bitterness; he wasted his money—we hoard it; he gave his body to prostitutes—we sacrifice our mind to pornography.

What ultimately saved the boy in the parable is that he came to despair of his life and began to crave what he had known at home. Many of us have never known that despair—but we should have. Someone put it like this, "Our churches are filled with nice, kind, loving people who have never known the despair of guilt or the breathless wonder of forgiveness."

Before we pray for them to come home, let's make sure they are really gone.

The only way the religious establishment could accuse Jesus of being a prodigal was because they had no idea of what really mattered to God. And it was for this reason they found it so hard to contemplate the awful possibility that in reality it was he who was in the Father's house and they who were left outside.

Before we pray for them to come home, let's make sure they are really gone.

Prayer

Lord, unclench my fist, my hand,
Pry open my fingers,
Break the habit of a lifetime
Years of comforting, providing.

Lord, release my thoughts,
Pry open my mind,
Let me trust you with this precious child.

Lord, have I trapped him by my love?
Too close, too tight?
Have I edged you out, forgetting
You knew him before he was born?
You loved him before I did?

He's yours, Lord,
I release him to you.

Reflection

Stop your crying and wipe away your tears.
All that you have done for your children will not go
unrewarded;
They will return from the enemy's land.
There is hope for your future;
your children will come back home.
I, the Lord, have spoken.

Jeremiah 31:16–17 *(Good News)*

God identifies with our tears at the absence of our prodigals. He shares them. But he promises us that all of our efforts and longings as parents, grandparents, husbands, wives, brothers, sisters, or friends do not go unnoticed by him. He assures us that he is in control and that he can be trusted with their lives, wherever they wander. There is hope.

Chapter Three

Before They Are Prodigals

A mother and father approached me during an event in North America at which I was speaking. They were in their early sixties, and their daughter was seventeen. The father said to me, "We're so worried about our daughter. She's always pushed the boundaries, but now she likes to go dancing on a Friday night."

"Well," I thought to myself, "at least she sounds normal."

The father went on, "Sometimes she likes to go dancing on a Saturday night as well."

"We're so worried about our daughter."

"You know," I said, "that's pretty ordinary behavior for a teenager. There are lots of dangers out there, but I've no doubt you've instilled in your daughter what's right and wrong, and in just a few months she'll be an adult."

The mother said, "But she refuses to go to the youth Bible study."

As they spoke I could imagine the scene in their house: this teenager coming downstairs and her parents saying, "You can't go out looking like that," or the arguments over whether she could go out again on Saturday having already been out on Friday night. My heart went out to this older couple who were doing all they could to keep their daughter on the right path but with the effort practically killing them.

"What's your daughter like around the house?" I asked.

"She's fine," the mother replied. "But as I said, she won't go to the youth Bible study."

"Does she ever go to church with you?" I asked, expecting them to say no, not since she was twelve.

They replied, "Every Sunday—she never misses."

"Do you mean to tell me that every Sunday, regardless of how late she comes home the night before, she is in church the next day?" I asked.

"Yes," they answered. "Every Sunday."

"That's incredible!" I said. "When you go home tonight I want you to say to your daughter, 'Darling, we were telling somebody about you tonight and the fact that you are so very faithful every Sunday in coming to church. We felt proud of you.'"

I will never forget what happened next. The mother looked at me and said, "Mr. Parsons, didn't you hear what we said a moment ago? She won't go to the youth Bible study!"

Praise her for what she is doing right.

"Forget that for the moment" I said. "Don't always be criticizing her for what you think she is doing wrong. Praise her for what she is doing *right*—because if you don't, you're going to have more to worry about than the youth Bible study. It seems to me that at the moment this child is trying to honor God as best she can, and she needs every encouragement in that. Don't make a prodigal of your daughter over some mid-week meeting."

Many families have a child who, in his or her younger years, looks likely to become a prodigal. I sometimes wonder if it becomes a self-fulfilling prophecy in that we set such impossible standards. We require him to jump through hoops he was never designed to negotiate, and eventually he gives up trying. He thinks to himself, "If my parents really think I'm so bad then I may as well prove them right."

> We require him to jump through hoops he was never designed to negotiate.

If you have more than one child, they will most likely be completely different from each other. If your first child is compliant, you may think you are the perfect parents—for a while. The first child loves helping with the dishes, spends hours tidying her room, and saves up her allowance to buy study guides. The second is a little different. This little boy wakes up every morning and says to himself, "How can I drive my mother crazy today?" He goes to bed worried that he hasn't done a good job of it.

In most homes you will find that the majority of the discipline, the sanctions, the curfews, and the arguments are centered on that more testing child. These actions may well be necessary, but there are dangers. I remember my son, Lloyd, saying to me when he was about sixteen years old, "Dad, I know it's not true now, but when I was young I used to think you loved Katie more than me."

"I understand that, son," I said, "because whenever pandemonium broke out you were in the middle of it, and in addition, I now realize that your big sister used to sneak some of her mischief onto you!"

It is imperative to find something in which we can encourage him.

We simply have to break the cycle where the only words such a child hears from us are negative. It is imperative to find something in which we can encourage him—perhaps let him overhear us praising him to others. It will help if we find something he can do well that his "Goody Two-Shoes" sibling can't. It may be a hobby or a sport—anything that gives him dignity in his own right. Work hard to find this skill in your child—it is absolutely vital. The alternative is for him or her to choose rebellion as the way of gaining a little significance. And, above all, we need to let this child know in a hundred ways that, although at times it seems to be constant warfare between us, we couldn't love him more.

And sometimes—even if our children are testing us to distraction—it's important to ask God to show us ways that He is already at work in the lives of our children so that we can encourage them: instead of constant criticism, actually catch them doing something *right*. Imagine next Saturday evening you are going to a special meeting at your church. You leave the house with your son. He is going downtown, and you fear for all he is going to experience that night. You know that although he says, "Don't wait up for me, Mom!" you won't go to sleep until you hear his key in the door. As you reach the street corner you part—you, to take the short walk to your church, and he, to catch the bus into the city center. He waves goodbye. You wave back and bite your bottom lip to stop the tears coming, and suddenly you witness something quite special. There is a homeless man selling magazines on the corner, and as you watch, your son takes some of his hard-earned money and buys a magazine. And then he does something few adults ever do; he actually touches the man on the arm, smiles, and says, "Keep the change, sir."

The next day you should wake up that boy (perhaps not before three in the afternoon!) and say, "When you did that, I was proud of you—and I believe that God was proud of you. It was the kind of thing that Jesus would have done." Some of our prodigals are not so far from God as we think. It is true they are a long way from our particular Christian culture—but not so far from God.

Ask God to show us ways that He is already at work in the lives of our children.

I remember having lunch with a company director and asking him to tell me about his family.

"I've got three kids" he replied. "My eldest daughter is twenty-five and she's doing a PhD; the second girl is twenty-two and she's doing an MA." With that he picked up his knife and starting eating. I said, "Tell me about your third child."

"Oh," he replied. "My son's nineteen. He's dyslexic. He doesn't work hard at college; his bedroom's a mess, and he gets parking tickets and forgets to pay them. I tell him he'd better sharpen up—it's a tough world out there."

I asked, "Can you remember when you last praised that boy for anything at all?"

He replied, "No, I really can't."

I said, "When you go home, find something that boy has done remotely well and praise him for it. It will revolutionize your relationship with him." To his credit he said that he would.

I think of another man who approached me at the end of a

business seminar. He told me that he had a very poor relationship with his nineteen-year-old daughter. I asked him what gifts his daughter had, and he replied that she was a fantastic singer. I asked him if he had ever told her he was proud of the way she sings. He replied, "Never." I urged him to do it that very day.

We all need to be praised more than we dare acknowledge.

We all need to be praised more than we dare acknowledge, and for our children, it is absolutely vital. It's good to know that even if your parents are on your back most of the time, you can, occasionally, make them proud.

The great danger for any parent is that the desire to let a child know how strongly we disapprove will be greater than the impulse that lets her know, no matter what she has done, she is still loved. I have heard parents in church making negative comments about their child's dress, facial piercings, or color of hair—and in front of that child. Maybe they are trying to say, "I know he looks like this/goes there/smokes, but I don't approve." Did we honestly think our friends thought all along that we were filled with enthusiasm for that pin through our daughter's lower lip? The price we pay for that little piece of self-justification is that our children come to believe that, although we tell them we love them, we actually don't *accept* them.

Unconditional love is one of the most powerful forces on the face of the earth.

I am always thrilled when I am in a church and notice a wild-looking teenager in the worship band. As I watch him play, I have no doubt in my mind that he would rather be backing a rock band, but nevertheless, this church has embraced this teenager as he is—and the way he looks, with the gifts he has—and said, "Be part of us. Bring your worship to God in your way."

Unconditional love is one of the most powerful forces on the face of the earth. But it can be very hard to give. One parent wrote:

> *I know there is no greater force than love, but we have loved our son until it has broken us. We have bailed him out of police cells and had drug dealers call at our home and threaten us. He has stolen from us, abused us, and brought us close to the edge of insanity. Sometimes we feel so guilty because we feel it would have been better if he had died. At least then he would be safe. But still we love. We cannot help loving. Only God can help us to love like that.*

There are some things we can do to help that more challenging child, but there's quite a lot we cannot do. Therefore, if we are wise, we will allow other adults—friends of ours, youth leaders, sports leaders—to play a part in molding our children's lives. It's hard because, especially during their teen years, our children may go through periods when they confide more readily in these "significant others" than in us. What can be even more galling is that they are happy to be seen walking down the street with these people—even though they may be as old and boring-looking as we are—but our children wouldn't be seen dead with us. The truth is that it's easier for these people—they don't have to deal with the twenty-four-hours-a-day pressures and hassles, or grapple with any discipline issues. Nevertheless their role is

Parenting is a long-haul business and our children may yet surprise us.

crucial. The breakdown in the extended family and the increasing isolation in which many families live have made such people harder to find—but find them we must.

But in the midst of it all, and whether right now our kids are easy to live with or whether they are driving us crazy, we would do well to remember that parenting is a long-haul business and our children may yet surprise us. And for that very reason we shouldn't read the score at halftime. That testing child can change, and the really big shock is that the compliant one may have a surprise or two up her sleeve—just enough to say, "Don't take me for granted. I can keep you awake at night as well."

And don't despair of sowing good seed into their lives. Even that more challenging child is taking in more than you think. One of the most encouraging and sobering aspects of parenting is not only how much our children remember of what we taught them, but that they actually eventually put it into practice in their own lives *as though they had thought of it themselves.*

Seeds sown in our children's lives . . . go deep into the soil of their very being.

If you doubt what I say then think how often you find yourself repeating advice that your parents once gave you which, somewhere between your teens years and however old you are now, moved from your disbelieving it, through to your ignoring it, to your finally not only adopting it as your own but actively promoting it as the best way to do things.

Seeds sown in our children's lives when they are small—Bible passages, stories of heroes and heroines of the faith, singing songs with them that can inspire them to faith in God—go deep into the soil of their very being. There are many prodigals who at their lowest moment remembered a line from an old hymn or a verse from the Bible that caused them to find hope again—and a way back. Don't be discouraged. Many a seed that seemed destined to die has somehow fought against rock and frost to find a way to life. My mother had green fingers. She could take a plant that others would have thrown on the rubbish heap and coax it back to life. Don't give up on that seed.

Remember the words of Jesus: "My Father is the gardener."

Prayer

Father God,
Look at my son.
He is unique—and how! There is no one else like
   him.
I cannot fathom him—or his ways.
But you know all of them.
You know his heart, his dreams.
If I have judged him by my standards instead of
   yours, forgive me.
If I have expected too much, been swift to criticize
   and slow to listen, I'm sorry.
Help me understand his way with you, and yours
   with him.
Help me accept that he does not need a pew to sit at
   your feet,
May not always need to do the done thing—just your
   thing,
That the songs he sings can be sung in a different
   tune.
I cannot watch his every move, plant his every step.
But your hand is on him wherever he goes
Until he really "comes home."

Reflection

Man looks at the outward appearance, but the Lord looks at the heart.

1 Samuel 16:7b

God often uses the most unconventional of his children in ways we could never have expected. His focus is the heart and motivation of those who claim to love and follow him, not their qualifications, charisma, or congeniality. Our ability to accept that God may act in surprising ways through surprising people—especially the young—is a measure of our spiritual maturity.

Pain is a language,
without words—
and so it is untouched
by words.

Does it help to know
that my prayers for you
are often wordless too?

And shaped like tears.

—Susan Lenzkes

We do not know what we ought to pray for, but the Spirit himself intercedes for us with groans that words cannot express . . .

Romans 8:26

Chapter Four

Letting Go of False Guilt

There is no pain like parental pain. The love of a parent for a child is like no other. Our children can disappoint us, hurt us, even abuse us, but somehow we cannot stop loving them. Sometimes it seems that the more they cause us to worry the more we love them. We would willingly give our lives for these children.

> The love of a parent for a child is like no other.

And yet sometimes that love can be very hard to give. I well remember a woman telling me that her thirteen-year-old daughter had driven her to despair. She said, "I hear other parents talk about the day when their kids leave home and the nest will be empty and yet I cannot wait for my daughter to go. I can't honestly tell you that I do *feel* love for this child." But something was driving this woman to tell her story to a stranger, and I am convinced it was a cry for help that said, "Help me to love this girl who, at times, I feel has ruined my life. She has broken my heart yet she is part of me—I cannot live without loving her."

And yet as much as we love them, as much as we want their good, as much as we would give all that we possess for their sakes, we cannot live their lives for them. Our children make choices. And sometimes those choices are bad ones.

We cannot live their lives for them.

A couple comes to my mind. They are church leaders and wonderful parents. Some years ago they sat with their sixteen-year-old daughter in a prison cell. She had just been arrested for burglary. I will never forget the simplicity of what they said to her in the cell that night: "Annie, you are breaking our hearts, but you will never stop us loving you."

I am sure that those parents would have willingly changed places with their child in that cell. But even if it had been possible, it might not have been for the best. We are their parents; we have spent all our lives making things right for them, but at times even we have to step back a little and let them learn the lessons of life. Sometimes the pain is part of the coming home.

But that doesn't stop us feeling that somehow we are responsible. The parable of the prodigal son is the third story of a trilogy. In the first there is a lost sheep, and in the second a lost coin. It would be hard to blame the sheep (and certainly the coin!) for getting lost, but this story is different. Here the boy is capable of making a decision and does so—to turn his back on the father and the father's house. He, himself, *chooses*. And yet in spite of the fact that our children make their own choices, we so often feel the guilt ourselves.

"Where did we go wrong?"

I have heard that guilt voiced by parents all across the world.

One couple will say, "Where did we go wrong? Would it be different if we'd been firmer with them?" Another will say, "Perhaps we were too rigid." A father will say, "If only we'd had daily devotions with our children," and another will say, "If only we *hadn't* had daily devotions with them. Perhaps we forced our faith on them too much." The guilt of those "if onlys" can be gut wrenching, all pervasive, and sometimes causes us to simply freeze in fear for our children.

We look at other families who seem to be doing so well. We meet people who say, "All four of my children are fantastic Christians" and we think, "It must be me. How come I got it so wrong?" And at times it seems so unfair. We see homes where the parents appear to have hardly bothered at all and yet their kids seem to be a cross between Mother Teresa and Hudson Taylor.

And sometimes the Christian community doesn't help a lot.

When David and Carla walked into church on that Sunday in June, they didn't exactly feel like worshiping but at least they were there. It had been a tough six months. Just after lunch on New Year's Eve their seventeen-year-old had declared that she was leaving home to live with a thirty-year-old man whom she had met at a Christmas party the week before. They

> And sometimes the Christian community doesn't help a lot.

had begged her not to go. In fact David had physically held her back in the hall of their home as she struggled, suitcase in hand, to get through the door. Louise had sworn, bitten, and kicked until one of their neighbors banged on the door to see what was happening. Finally David and Carla had no choice. As they watched her get into the car they both sank to the floor and cried until it got dark.

Two months later their son, aged nineteen, called from the university to say he was quitting his course. He and his girlfriend had decided to hitchhike around Europe for a while.

The preacher that Sunday was a visitor. He began by telling the congregation about his family. He had been married for twenty-seven years and had four children between the ages of eighteen and twenty-five. All were, as he put it, "walking with the Lord" and doing well in their studies, two of them already training for missionary service overseas. Carla didn't hear a word of the sermon. She was too busy thinking, "When did it start to unravel?" "Where did we go wrong?" and "How can I get out of this church without talking to anybody?"

"How can I get out of this church without talking to anybody?"

There are thousands of parents who feel like this. Parents of teenagers, parents of twenty-somethings, and elderly parents whose middle-aged children are still managing to break their hearts. And sometimes the hurt can come out of a clear blue sky. Like the father who told me this:

My wife and I had just come out of church on a Sunday morning when my cell phone rang. It was my best friend calling from a police station to tell me my son had just been arrested. I felt my knees give way. As my friend handed his phone to my son and I waited for him to come on the line I remember thinking, "I've got just one chance to get this right."

I could hear my son crying on the other end of the phone. My first reaction was to yell at him, but the words I actually spoke seemed to belong to somebody else. "Son, I am ashamed

*of what you have done but I am not ashamed of you. I love
you. With God's help we will come through this."*

And as if parenting wasn't hard enough anyway, modern so-
ciety practically forces us to see our children's lives as a judgment
on whether or not *we* have been successful. We want our children
to do well because we want to be well-thought-of ourselves. So
often, when our children go through tough times—whether it's
unexpectedly poor grades or some much more serious issue—our
first thought is, "What will people think
of us?"

One church leader, realizing that
this was happening to him, put it like
this: "My boy is going through a hard
time right now and my main concern is,
'What will my congregation think?' But
I only have just enough emotional energy
to deal with the real issues, and I've decided that I have to set myself free of what others think. The greatest need is my son's well
being, not my reputation."

> "The greatest need is my son's well being, not my reputation."

Only more honesty among us will set us free from the tyranny
of the fear of what others will think; only less judging, more praying, and the realization that God, the *perfect* parent, is a *hurting*
parent. All of us would do well not to crow too loudly when our
kids are doing well. Marie Anne Blakely put it well: "A mother is
neither proud nor arrogant because she knows that any moment
the headmaster may ring to say that her son has just ridden a mo-
torcycle through the school gymnasium."

Some years ago Dr. R.T. Kendall, then the senior minister at
Westminster Chapel in London, was asked by the Billy Graham
organization if they could film him for an hour talking about the-

ology. Dr. Kendall talked to the camera about some of the issues he used to tackle in his Friday evening School of Theology classes. When they got to the end the producer said, "We've got five minutes of film left. Would you talk to us about your family?" Dr. Kendall, who could be blunt to a fault, replied, "You don't want to know about my family. I've been a failure as a father."

"I've been a failure as a father."

I believe that R.T., as we call him, is a wonderful father, but it was his view that when his children were young he devoted too much time to his studies and to Westminster Chapel. At the time the film was made you could say that his children were prodigals. However the producer begged him to continue, and so R.T. talked about those years and the mistakes he felt he had made.

The only part of the film the producers ever used—and they showed it to thousands of church leaders all across the world—was those last few minutes. It was utterly compelling. It said to others going through heartbreaking times—this is not just you.

It's no surprise they used the film in that way. I well remember hearing Dr. Billy Graham talk of the years when his son Franklin was a prodigal. He said, "Ruth and I lived in a house on top of a hill, and some nights we would lie awake in the early hours of the morning waiting for Franklin to come home. Finally we would hear the car screeching its way around the bends as it came up the mountain, and we would know, at least for one more night, he was safe."

So many parents are carrying a heavy load of guilt they have no need to bear.

So many parents are carrying a heavy load of guilt they have no need to bear. That's not to say they have been perfect parents. They have just been *parents*—parents who have given this task their very best efforts. There's hardly a mother or father on the face of the earth who wouldn't love to have another shot at parenting—to rewind the clock and get the chance to read all the books and go to all the seminars before their children hit the teenage years. But even if we had that chance, the truth is we'd probably just make different mistakes.

And what if we could have been the *perfect* parents? The creation story brings a fascinating dimension to this. Adam and Eve had the perfect father and lived in the perfect environment, but they chose a way their father didn't want them to go. In fact much of the Bible shows God, the perfect parent, saying to his children, "Why are you turning your back on all that I have taught you?" There are no guarantees with our children. I know there is that verse in Proverbs, "Bring up a child in the way he should go and when he is old he will not depart from it," but that's not a guarantee, it's a general principle. If you follow it, you will give your children a wonderful foundation in life, but they will still make choices. And sometimes those choices are bad.

It's time to lay that guilt down. You have carried it long enough. By all means ask forgiveness for those things you know you've done wrong as a parent, but then join the rest of us who have loved and guided our children as much as we could, but who, in the end, have to watch as they make their own decisions.

It's time to lay that guilt down.

There is nothing so soul-destroying as false guilt. Let it go. And begin to ask God the Father to reach out to your prodigals as only he can. Ultimately they are in his hands not ours.

And, in truth, it was always so.

Ask God the Father to reach out to your prodigal.

Prayer

Lord,
I have only ever loved her.

You know how that feels. To give a child everything
   and watch them throw it all away.
Sometimes the guilt causes me to cry myself to sleep,
And when I wake, it is in my stomach.

I rewind the past and ask, "What could we have
   done?"
Or sometimes, "What if I hadn't . . . ?"

I watch others who are proud, sometimes, it seems,
   even boastful of their children,
Although I would not rob them of a moment of their
   pleasure.

Cut me free from what others might think or say.
From the pain of hearing them congratulate
   themselves for the way their children have "turned
   out."
As if the mold she has fallen from was a "second."
Help me find a place with those who understand and
   have known this pain.

I need you to whisper to me that I did my best,
I was not perfect but I gave what I could.
And, Lord, even where I failed you can mend.
If I wounded, you can heal.

Heal me, Lord.
Lift this guilt.
Now.

Reflection

They felt good eyes upon them
and shrank within—undone;
good parents had good children
and they—a wandering one.

The good folk never meant
to act smug or condemn,
but having prodigals
just "wasn't done" with them.

Remind them gently, Lord,
how you
have trouble with Your children,
too.

Ruth Bell Graham

The time comes when we can no longer stagger forward with the burden guilt places on us. It is then that we must remember that God, the perfect Father, has wayward children.

Our children are ultimately God's responsibility. He is their Father. He does not ask the impossible of us. Only that we love them.

As you pray now, turn and kneel at the foot of the cross, lay down the guilt, and the crippling fear. Let God hold you.

CHRIS'S STORY

I'm now in my mid-twenties. At age five I sat on the dropped lid of a toilet and prayed with my Dad crouching beside me. It was the only quiet place we could find to ask God to come into the life of a curious, average boy with Christian parents. I remember few details except the size of the room and the fact my feet hardly touched the wooden floors. But I remember knowing that this was a big deal, I knew God was real. A few years later I dropped and surfaced in a baptism pool, watching bubbles chase above me, trying to remember every moment in perfect detail for later reference. When I spoke in front of the assembled church I declared Jesus publicly as God, as my God. I did what thousands of Christians have been persecuted for in the safest place I could, and it was real. I didn't lie to the minister, my family, or the little old ladies in the front row. And most of all I didn't lie to him. I didn't worry about tomorrow; as promised, tomorrow brought enough of it's own.

After that point, life got thick and fast, fun and tempting; it became difficult to focus on a life which promised its rewards elsewhere. Where the church prescribed a code of conduct and an argument in support, it seemed the world had laid out life in all its fullness with all the trimmings. I was a normal teenager; I was more than a little torn.

The author Hanif Kureishi, recounting his own experience, concluded that "Being a child at all involves resolving, or synthesizing, at least two different worlds, outlooks, and positions—one way of coping would be to reject one world entirely, perhaps by forgetting it. Another is to be at war with it internally, trying to evacuate it, but never succeeding." I fought that war for many years, unwilling to reject either of those two worlds. One, because it was too beautiful and tragic, it offered too much; the other, because deep down I knew it was real. God had been here, walked this earth, and wanted more from me—I believed that much. However, I felt no nearer to him in the corporate gatherings of his followers than I did walking the streets at night. I didn't see God in church or nature or anywhere at all. I hung in there, still around church, still part of the youth group, if only in body but not spirit. Sermons washed over me like TV commercials; I saw no examples of Christians I aspired to be like, and the Bible was to me a confusing anthology of badly written morality tales. But at the hub of all this rejection, and even below a thin surface of resentment, was an unimpressive but solid sense that this was all true.

Even he slipped by unnoticed. The Jesus that I would later find so compelling managed to avoid my attention throughout every sermon my childhood notched up. I missed that fathomless, unpredictable man. I failed to notice the king who touched the poor and said he'd come to serve them, the revolutionary who turned down a plausible rebellion and opted for one which meant going silently to his grave. The perfect man who set unreasonable standards, who commanded his hangers-on to be as perfect as his father was, and yet, met their inevitable failures with unmeasured forgiveness. Now, he is my reason for forward motion; then, all I had was a two-dimensional cardboard cut-out, meek, mild, and totally voiceless.

The period in my life when I was at university was probably the furthest that I have ever been from God, I expect many have found the same. I made it through most of it without giving God a second thought. But towards the end of my time, I would find myself awake in the middle of the night or caught off guard with my thoughts straying onto something bigger than the sum of what my life added up to. Eventually after finishing my degree and leaving the country I met

God six thousand miles from home, in the last place I expected to find him. It turns out he likes to chase.

Working with some very poor young people, I found myself challenged about the system of values I had discreetly created, and I decided that I wanted to know what a life worth living looked and felt like. On Sunday mornings I found myself rolling up to the church where some of my colleagues went. Often I would go to services in the local slums, and it seemed at every moment someone around me was talking about God. In a short space of time I found myself part of a small group of people whom I could relate to, despite our different backgrounds, nationalities and levels of faith, and whether we were leaning over a beer or an open Bible. Reading that book I found a man worth following and with him a hundred questions about whether I really could. I found a community of people willing to listen, looking outwards, and wanting to know God better today than they did yesterday. I saw church how it was intended to be.

Today, I co-lead an "experimental" church plant in a city-center pub in my spare time. Essentially it's a church for people who don't like what they have seen of "church," and we get a variety of types. Some have had no previous Christian contact in their life; others have and were either mistreated or didn't "fit in." As you can imagine, they bring their questions and frustrations, they are totally uninterested in church culture, unfazed by our attempts to be "relevant," but they are interested in Jesus, and the question of whether he is. But there's another group, a group of people retesting the Christian faith, those that have heard it all before and have gone away only to find that nothing else out there makes sense. They've been there, they have the T-shirt, and they want something more. Most will have a moment in their life when they realize they're in a pig pen and they want to go home. I have a lot of time for prodigals. I've seen what

God can do when they come back.

If I've learned anything, it's that God is totally concerned with us. We are unique. Your fourteen-year-old son or daughter who won't talk to you over the supper table is unique (you may not find that hard to believe) and is the total preoccupation of God. Sometimes it's helpful to remind ourselves of that. Too often we can read the story of the prodigal son and forget that it is allegorical. The temptation is to think of it only as an example of how we should forgive our children, forgetting that it's actually an example of how God forgives his. This stands as a lesson about how God waits, and the kind of party he throws when we come home.

I believe that God has great things in store for prodigals. He wants to mold them, but not crush their personalities. He wants them to bring their talents, experiences, and their new-found passion, as well as their questions and frustrations, and put them to work in the family business—the kingdom of heaven, here and now, then and forever.

Chapter Five

Stop Judging and Start Sharing

One of the clearest recollections of my life when I was young is of a church meeting on a September evening. For the previous few years there had been an undercurrent of dissatisfaction with the leadership, and now it was all coming to a head. This was high noon and the flock were going to tell the shepherds exactly what they thought. And some of them did—including a man who told one of the leaders that because the leader's teenage son was going through a rebellious time, he was not fit to lead the church. I can remember watching the leader answer as graciously as he possibly could, but his embarrassment was evident for all to see.

> His embarrassment was evident for all to see.

A silence descended on the meeting. It was as if we knew something was happening that was either wrong or foolish. In truth it was both. The man who spoke had made two mistakes: first, with his interpretation of the Bible, and second, his own children were toddlers at the time. If you are going to criticize anyone else's children, you should always wait until your own are in their nineties—anything less exposes you to the possibility of a diet of your own words. Kids change. So whether they are at present breaking our hearts or seem like visiting angels, it's best to remember that, in the words of one of America's greatest baseball players, Yogi Berra, "It ain't over till it's over."

"It ain't over till it's over."

That kind of judgment comes easily, because there are times in the Christian community when we give the impression that if we follow a certain set of guidelines it will guarantee our children will turn out to be everything we ever hoped for. A friend of mine was recently asked to give a sermon entitled "How to Bring up Godly Children."

Are there really steps we can take, programs we can follow, or biblical injunctions that we can adopt that will help us build a strong foundation for our children's lives? Yes, there are.

Is it possible to teach our children lessons about God, others, and themselves that will stand them in good stead through the whole of their lives? Of course.

Can we co-operate with the Holy Spirit in doing our part as parents to help our children love God and want to serve him? Absolutely.

But we cannot, and we are fools if we think we can, do certain acts, parent in a certain way, even pray certain prayers, that allow us to say categorically: "*This* is how to bring up godly children."

There are parents who have got it more right than most but whose children have turned their back on everything they hold dear, and there are those who have got it more wrong than most whose children serve God faithfully today. You and I cannot bring up godly children; it is not our responsibility—it is too heavy a burden. We are called instead to live godly lives.

I remember a Christian leader's wife saying to me some years ago, "Considering your involvement with Care for the Family, wouldn't it be ironic if your kids went off the rails?"

I may have imagined it, but as she spoke I thought I saw a glint of hope in her eyes that they *would*. I replied, "It wouldn't be ironic at all. My wife Dianne and I have given the task of parenting our very best shot but there are no guarantees."

As I said earlier, Dianne and I thank God for every bit of evidence we see in our kids' lives that God is at work, but I could not have written this book if there had never been a time when we had cried over them. What I said all those years ago in reply to that woman is still true—there are no guarantees. Our children, as do all of us, follow Christ a day at a time, with many a fall, and every step by the mercy of God.

The time has come to let the masks drop.

Many of us need to repent of the way we have judged other people's children and instead begin to support each other. The time has come to let the masks drop, to begin to say "me too," and to set each other free from the intolerable burden of being the perfect parents. The wonderful thing is that when we are honest with each other, when we pray for each others' children, then their successes are not a threat to us but a joy—for they bring us hope for our own kids.

Some time ago I received this letter. The father who wrote it told me to use it to bring encouragement to others:

Last November our two eldest children, Brian and James, were convicted of crimes and both received prison sentences. My wife and I have tried to bring up our children on Christian principles, so it came as a very big shock when our sons followed this lifestyle.

> ## It came as a very big shock when our sons followed this lifestyle.

Brian is in a young offenders' prison, and James is in an adult prison, which means that they have been separated since conviction.

Although for a while our sons' lifestyles have been very different from ours, we have remained a close family. We have a daughter, Carol, aged fifteen, and we all have visited as much as we can. Brian and James seldom ask for others to use their visit allowance.

We have not met any parents in our situation, so we have not been able to learn directly from the experience of others, but we have a very supportive church family. One thing that we believe has been key, and led by God, has been our honesty and openness in talking about this. We kept the church informed and told our employers and colleagues about our sons' trouble. I felt it was important that I did not keep it a secret from my work-mates; they were my friends, and they knew my family and cared about us.

> ## Our strength has come from our honesty.

So many people told us that they admired our bravery, but what we feel is that our strength has come from our honesty rather than us having the *strength to be brave. God encouraged us to be open, and he has carried us through this situation in a way that we have been able to encourage others. We have had people confide in us of situations they have kept hidden and carried as burdens for years, and we are so grateful that God has spared us from that.*

I know that we can't wear our hearts on our sleeves with everybody, and the truth is that some people simply won't be able to handle what we may be going through with our children, but there will be other hurting parents in your church, and certainly in your neighborhood, with whom you can share. Meet with them, pray with them, laugh and cry with them. The Bible says we should "bear one another's burdens." That means to actually lighten the load. But there is an important qualification we must have if we are to do it. It was Thornton Wilder who said, "In love's service, only the wounded soldiers can serve."

It has always been so in the kingdom of God.

Prayer

Lord, forgive the way we've judged each other.
We've all done it.
At times when our family life was going well,
Commented, carped, and sometimes enjoyed too
 much the giving of advice.
Well, Lord, now all that is gone.
We have no illusions about our right to preach, or
 teach, or criticize.
We have cried, are wounded now ourselves.
Lord, don't let this pain be wasted.
Let it rather cause us to go to those we might have
 criticized
And throw our arms around them, hold them near.
As we sustain each other and cry out together from
 broken hearts,
"Lord, have mercy."

Reflection

Praise be to the God and Father of our Lord Jesus Christ, the Father of compassion and the God of all comfort, who comforts us in all our troubles, so that we can comfort those in any trouble with the comfort we ourselves have received from God.

2 Corinthians 1:3–4

"In love's service, only the wounded soldiers can serve." Those who have been wounded and live with the scars often have the greatest understanding of the pain of others. It is more than having an experience in common, or showing empathy. It can be a "fellowship of suffering." We feel bound to one another by invisible, but invincible cords.

The knowledge that another understands our pain can be liberating. The pain may not go away, but suddenly it becomes bearable.

Thank God for someone with whom you share, or have shared, a fellowship of suffering, or pray that he will bring someone alongside you with whom you can discover it.

Chapter Six

Releasing the Power of Forgiveness

If love is the greatest power on the face of the earth, then forgiveness is the second greatest. Without forgiveness we die inside. With it, the memories may still be there but we can at least begin to move on. But for those who cry for prodigals there are often so many things to forgive.

Sometimes we have to forgive those who have hurt the ones we love. My deepest gratitude and lifelong debt is to those who have been there for my children, and my deepest wounds have been at the hands of those who have hurt them. We may blame others for being part of our prodigals' rebellion, for being judgmental when they should have been supportive, for the comments they made to us at our lowest moments when we

> ### Without forgiveness we die inside.

so desperately needed their comfort, but we must forgive them—even if that person is our husband or wife. We must stop nursing the hurt. We have to let it go.

And although we love them, we sometimes still have to forgive our prodigals, for they may have treated us badly. They may have thrown our love, care, and most fervent desire for their good straight back in our faces. And we must forgive even while they are still hurting us. We may want to say, "If only he would stop that lifestyle, or give up the drink or the drugs," or "If only she would get rid of the man who seems to be draining her of life, then we would forgive," but we must forgive even when there is no evidence that they may change.

> **We must forgive even when there is no evidence that they may change.**

What is the alternative to forgiveness? It is rejection. And rejection often brings with it isolation, bitterness, and a pushing even further away of those we are trying to draw back. One young man wrote to his parents that he was going to marry his fiancée with or without their approval. He may have been both headstrong and insensitive, but even so, the letter he got back from his father took his breath away. It read: "Don't worry about inviting us to the wedding. We no longer have a son."

Forgiveness allows us to go on loving. There is no greater exhibition of love than the death of Jesus, but that love could flow only because even as they were still banging nails into his hands and feet he cried out, "Father, forgive them." Forgiveness is not Disney World. Forgiveness finds itself in the real world of deep hurts, dashed

> **Forgiveness allows us to go on loving.**

hopes, and broken promises. But there is no hope for our prodigals without it.

Ernest Hemingway wrote a short story set in Spain in which a father and son fell out to such an extent that the son ran away to Madrid. The father said he wanted nothing more to do with him. Years later, the father realized he had been too harsh and wanted to put things right. He put an ad in a Madrid newspaper: "Paco, meet me at the Hotel Montana at noon on Tuesday. All is forgiven. Papa."

But Paco is a common name in Spain, and when the father turned up at the hotel he had to force his way through a crowd: all young men, all called Paco—and all longing to be reconciled with their father.

Of course, there may be another who needs forgiveness, for in spite of all I have said about being free of guilt there are moments when we may feel we have wronged our children—that our behavior has been part of their being in some "distant country." Perhaps it was our legalism, our controlling nature, or the affair we had that drove them away. Whatever we have done, we must ask for God's forgiveness, and then for the forgiveness of our prodigals. It may be hard to ask the forgiveness of someone who is hurting you so much, but it is such a powerful thing to do. Sometimes it robs our prodigals of the very reason for their rebellion.

> Whatever we have done, we must ask for God's forgiveness.

A mother wrote to me:

Sharon was a classic defiant toddler who grew into a defiant teenager. She took any boundary as a personal insult! We had always been close, but with the teen hormones tur-

bo-charging her drive for independence, she and I had what amounted to trench warfare for about ten years. Our relationship became seriously damaged. She felt I no longer loved her, and out of my own fears and concern I, for the most part, communicated disapproval.

Things came to a head when one day she told us she was pregnant. I was utterly devastated and felt a huge sense of failure. She moved out of our home to live with her partner. Things between us were at an all-time low.

Then while on holiday, I took up someone's suggestion to write her a letter. Over four pages I apologized, explained, and re-affirmed my love for her. For her own good I did not want her spending years living in reaction and bitterness against me.

I was in tears as I wrote the letter.

I was in tears as I wrote the letter. She cried as she read it. Our relationship became completely healed. Things were said in the letter that we could not easily have said face-to face. Important things. Chloe, our grand-daughter, has just turned three. She is a delight. Strong willed like her mother but a wonderful gift to us all. Out of all our children, Sharon is the one most like me—cut from the same quarry. It has felt at times that we were pre-programmed to clash in the way we did.

This is a story of restoration and hope; of how things that are incredibly painful can be healed. I have learned some important lessons, and now I see that I failed those lessons first time around. Maybe others can learn from my mistakes.

Sometimes the prodigals are there because a phone call needs to be made, or a letter written. Maybe others could find hope in our story.

With warm regards,

Sylvia Clarkson

God's grace will allow us to do the hardest thing of all—to forgive ourselves.

Finally, then, God's grace will allow us to do the hardest thing of all—to forgive ourselves. And when that happens the parable suddenly comes alive in a new way, for as we look at the figure coming down the road, we suddenly see that the dirty, tear-stained face is *our* face; it is *we* who are coming home full of shame and hearing the Father say, "Put a robe on his back, shoes on his feet, and a ring on his finger." It is then that we discover what, deep in our heart, we knew all along:

We are the prodigal.

Prayer

Gracious God,

Give us the grace to forgive our child.

To let go of the hurt, the broken promises, the
unfulfilled dreams.

For without forgiveness love will die, when it must
live.

The future will be filled with bitterness, when it must
be filled with hope.

As they mock, pour scorn, and steal our very dignity,
help us forgive.

For if they don't know our forgiveness, they will not
know our love.

And our love may be all they have.

Father, help us forgive them—for they know not
what they do.

Reflection

If we claim to be without sin we deceive ourselves and the truth is not in us. If we confess our sins, he is faithful and just and will forgive us our sins and purify us from all unrighteousness.

1 John 1:8–9

How great is the love the Father has lavished on us, that we should be called children of God.

1 John 3:1–2

"We are so busy being parents that we forget that all along what God wants most from us is for us to be his children."
"And it is then we discover what, deep in our heart, we knew all along: We are the prodigal."

You can always come home

As you pray for the prodigals who are on your heart you may like to reflect on the following letter, written by a mother who is a friend of mine. You may even make it your own and send it.

You might be surprised to hear from me. It is some time since we spoke, even longer since we were together. But I have rewound and reworded our last conversation and re-lived our last meeting many times in my heart and imagination.

Words passed between us that would have been best left unsaid. Others could have built bridges across which to reach each other but were dismissed before they ever reached our lips. I painfully regret both.

But not all the memories are painful. I often wind the tape back further like video film and watch you as a child, clambering on a rocky beach, or running with an excited smile to show me some treasure. I can still feel your hand in mine as you urged me to hurry along a windy street or held me back because you wanted to watch a tiny insect on an even slower journey. I remember you as you grew. The challenges you faced and the friends you made. The pride I felt.

Then I wonder when things started to go wrong? When we stopped talking and started shouting? When even the shouting gave way to silence, and the silence to absence?

You have walked a path in these last days that I would not have chosen for you. But, as you often said, it is your life and you must choose for yourself, and I have accepted those choices, however different they might be from my own.

I want you to know that my love for you is greater than those differences. That despite all that has built a barrier between us, the love I have for you is strong enough to move it, even if piece by piece, and however long it takes.

Both of us need the forgiveness of the other. We still need to hear the words we've longed for. I believe it's never too late.

You may choose to ignore these words. They may make you angry, rekindling memories that you thought you had long forgotten. I understand that. But as your mother I can do nothing but go on loving you, go on asking for your forgiveness, and offering mine to you. No matter what has happened in the past and whatever is going on in your life right now, I love you, I am here for you, and you can always come home.

Chapter Seven

When the Father's House Is Filled with the Father's Love . . .

I will never forget a prophecy given by an old man: "When the Father's house is filled with the Father's love, the prodigals will come home." If he is right, then perhaps the greatest obstacle to the return of our prodigals is the state of the church.

All across the world churches are fighting each other—not just denominational or inter-church disputes, but fighting within local churches. The other day I met a senior pastor from a church many miles from where I live. I asked him how he was. "Oh, not good; there's trouble in the church."

I interrupted before he could explain: "Let me tell you about it."

"But you've never even visited my church!"

> "There's trouble in the church."

"I know," I said. "But I have spoken to tens of thousands of church leaders all across the world. I can tell you what the trouble is about: it's probably either about the building program, the style of worship, or the youth work."

"How did you know that?"

I was on a roll. "I can tell you more than that," I said. "There's a small group of people who come up to you at the end of a Sunday service and say: 'Pastor, lots of us are worried about x or y.' And you say, 'Well, who are all these worried people?' And they say, 'Oh, I can't give you names!'"

It was the last night of Jesus' life: within twenty-four hours he would be dead and buried. And he said to those who were with him: "Love each other as I have loved you." No amount of church growth, building programs, or strategy can count for much if we do not strive for this love. It is said that when John, the last of the twelve to die, was old and weak, his friends would carry him into church meetings. As they did, he would say, "Love each other, love each other."

"Love each other as I have loved you."

"You always say the same to us," they said. "Have you nothing new?"

And he would reply, "It is enough. It was the Lord's command."

When I meet people who have decided to stop attending church they rarely tell me it is because of some crisis of faith or disappointment with God. No, it is much more likely that they will talk about relationships within that church and sometimes of the person who hurt them deeply. This is never easy to deal with because it is possible they expected too much of others and, of course, are rarely without blame themselves. Nevertheless we have somehow made it hard for them to stay and sometimes almost impossible for them to return.

One of the most sobering aspects of local church life is the realization that the way we have dealt with each other has caused some of our children to turn their back on what we believe. Through much of their young lives they have seen Christians fight each other and argue over the insignificant. They have silently watched as church members, including, perhaps, their parents, have criticized each other, hurt each other, and ostracized those they were meant to love. We forget that such attitudes make it very hard for others to follow Christ. One of Jesus' final prayers was: "Father, I pray that they may be one, that the world may believe that you sent me."

> We have somehow made it hard for them to stay.

There is something mystical about the way Christians relate to each other that authenticates the very love of God to people, and yet it is in the area of love at the local church level that there is often such difficulty. Wherever I travel I find churches splitting. There are arguments over styles of worship, youth programs, or building schemes. Many leave their local church and join another, only to leave the new church after a few years because that one, too, has failed to meet their demands.

Some of us have developed a critical spirit in our dealings with others, which makes it hard for our children to believe that God can love unconditionally. I urge parents not to criticize church leaders or other members of church in front of their young children. There is many a Sunday lunch table filled with conversation about what is wrong with the preaching, the music, or how hopeless the youth leader is.

You and I do not have the right to belong to a church that suits us in every respect. The great tragedy of much of church life today is that we have come to believe that "church is for us." We may have evangelistic programs and a myriad of other activities but in our hearts we have a view of what suits us, and woe betide the leadership if we don't get it. But it was never meant to be like this among us. This is how Paul describes the quality of relationship that demonstrates to a broken world the very love of God:

> *Love from the center of who you are. . . . Be good friends who love deeply; practice playing second fiddle. . . . Bless your enemies; no cursing under your breath. Laugh with your happy friends when they're happy; share tears when they're down. Get along with each other; don't be stuck up. Make friends with nobodies; don't be the great somebody. Don't hit back; discover beauty in everyone. If you've got it in you, get along with everybody. Don't insist on getting even; that's not for you to do. "I'll do the judging," says God. "I'll take care of it."*

Romans 12 (*The Message*)

> ## Some of us have developed a critical spirit in our dealings with others.

> ## "Be good friends who love deeply."

I think now of a teenage girl whose experience of church wasn't like that at all. In fact she saw her father, the church leader, driven to a nervous breakdown because of the pressure of dealing with bitter and sustained criticism. When Lucy, at age sixteen, vowed never to darken the door of a church again, it wasn't God she was turning her back on; it was the local church.

The scary thing about bringing up children is they so easily catch our values. They watch the way we deal with each other and draw from that a view of how God deals with us. If

> It wasn't God she was turning her back on; it was the local church.

you want children to grow up to believe that God could never love them if they get it wrong, then let them hear you pull apart the daughter of one of the church leaders who has just gotten pregnant. There are many prodigals who have gone even further away because, on the basis of what they saw in their young years in church, they believed that once you fell, there was no way back. The opposite is also true. When they see us try to stand for truth with compassion and utter love, they come to believe this is how God will act towards them.

My mind goes to a situation where a church leader was discovered to have had a severe lapse of moral judgment. The newspapers were full of the story, and Christians too seemed to be having a field day talking about where he had gone wrong. The ten-year-old daughter of another church leader came home from church one Sunday and said to her father, "Dad, people in church are saying that man has done really bad things." Her father thought for a moment and then replied, "Darling, he *has*

> "I want her to know there is always a way back."

done bad things, but if he honestly asks for God's forgiveness then God will gladly welcome him home."

That leader said to me later, "When my daughter spoke to me about it that day it was practically a holy moment. Of course I disapprove of what this man has done, but if I joined in with the condemnation, what would that have said to my daughter if ever she falls? I want her to know there is always a way back."

If you would be truly radical, then do what Jesus said and invite your enemies to your parties. Be more tolerant of differences among each other; stop gossiping, and "Don't bad-mouth each other, friends. It's God's Word, his Message, his Royal Rule, that takes a beating in that kind of talk. You're supposed to be honoring the Message, not writing graffiti all over it."

(James 4:11, The Message).

A couple of years ago I was conducting a seminar for church leaders. In the interval I saw an Anglican vicar who looked distressed. I asked him if he was all right. He turned to me with tears in his eyes, "It's just that when you spoke about criticism it moved me greatly. I'm going through a tough time at the moment with a small group of people in our church. One woman who acts as spokesperson has just written me a letter with thirty things that are wrong with the church."

"What did you do when you got the letter?" I asked.

"I answered every one of the issues she raised."

I told him I didn't think that was a good idea. He asked why and I said, "Because she wasn't satisfied, was she?"

He smiled ruefully, "No. She's

The only problem is: their prodigals won't come home.

just written me with another twenty!"

If they stamp and kick for it, that little group may well get the church of their dreams. They will get the kind of building they want, the style of teaching they want. They will achieve the style of worship they prefer—whether it is swinging from the chandeliers or using the old green hymn book. They can have the youth leader they want, and the color of carpet they want, and the flowers on the altar they want. They can have it all.

The only problem is: their prodigals won't come home.

·

Prayer

Lord, we repent of the state of your house.
Your dying prayer was that, above all, it should be
    filled with love.
We have filled it with programs, meetings, minutes,
    and agendas,
But the love is hard to see sometimes.

What things we do to one another.
How easily we gossip, slander, stamp, and kick to get
    our way,
And wound those you have died for.
Sometimes it is easier to survive the world outside
    than your church within.

Forgive us. And especially forgive us if our criticism,
    our biting tongues, our lack of love,
Have made it easier for some soul to leave your
    house—or harder to return.

And help us to change. To lay aside the judging, and
    the petty fights and squabbles
And lay a table, make a feast, pin some ribbons on
    the door.

And yell into the darkness of the night, "Give us
another chance—to love you and each other.
The house is not perfect, but it is swept and cleaned,
and a lamp is lit.
Come home."

Reflection

Father, the time has come. . . . My prayer is not for them alone. I pray also for those who will believe in me through their message, that all of them may be one, Father, just as you are in me and I am in you. May they also be in us so that the world may believe that you have sent me.

John 17:1, 20–21

Within twenty-four hours of this prayer, Jesus was both dead and buried.

"When the Father's house is filled with the Father's love the prodigals will come home."

What can I do in my local church to increase this love and hasten their return?

JULIE'S STORY

When I was fourteen my parents, who were hard-working and, I suppose, what you might call "dynamic" church leaders, moved our family abroad to take up a new job in church leadership. I found it really hard to leave my old school and friends. I felt vulnerable and very insecure. There were lots of problems. The other kids in my school were stinking rich, while we weren't. Everyone hung out together after school, smoking cigarettes. I felt totally out of it. I needed acceptance and couldn't compete. Being a Christian felt so difficult and so irrelevant, and that's when things started to go wrong, the beginning of me getting lost. I remember being in a café with about five other girls and asking for a cigarette. They wouldn't let me have one unless I learned how to inhale. The irony was that they didn't want me to waste their cigarettes.

I stayed at that school for two years and then went to another one. That was hell. I remember I used to cake myself in white make-up, both to hide and to blend in with the others.

When I went to college to do A-levels, I met a girl—Karen. She was cool. I don't know what it was. I remember having a conversation with her at school, and for some reason I thought she wouldn't be a virgin. So I told her that, of course, I'd lost my virginity at fifteen, and that's when the lying started. I began to develop a secret life away from my parents. I was sinking. Not able to compete and be perfect, feeling like rubbish academically, and a complete failure. It drove me into hiding in a different world.

Karen and I had "fun"—kissing boys, clubbing. I remember one time Dad coming up to my bedroom, sitting on the edge of my bed and telling me he didn't want me to go clubbing. I was saying, "No, of course not," but secretly thinking, "Oops, hope he doesn't find out

I went last night." Looking back it was awful. Karen had the use of her father's credit cards and, well, I just used to lie to my parents in order to be able to go out and enjoy our outrageous lifestyle.

Karen got me into modeling as well. She had all this expensive photography gear, so she took seventy-two shots of me sprawled over park benches—provocative headshots, pouty sexy shots. I remember taking them back and showing Mom and Dad who then promptly confiscated them, saying that they were pornographic. Looking back, they probably were. They weren't beautiful; I looked ill and unhappy; too thin.

I was doing really badly at college. The only friends I had seemed to be Karen and boyfriends. They didn't care about me though. I didn't know how to communicate with my parents; my denials and deceit had put up a huge barrier between us, so I kept running away.

I started skipping school. I spent days in a row trawling round the city just so I didn't have to go to school and sit at lunch on my own and face the consequences of not having done my homework. I sat in cafes, with hardly any money. The days were so long. I missed the deadline for displaying my A-level artwork because I thought it was just rubbish and nearly failed. My spiritual life was non-existent. My relationship with my parents was all lies, and I saw no way out— there were many times when I just didn't go home. And yet my parents were trying so hard to show me their love for me; I would often come home to notes from Mom. Unfortunately I was past knowing how to communicate. I felt dirty and sad. So it went on.

One day I ran away, and the person who I'd gone to stay with felt so guilty about Mom and Dad not knowing where I was that she called them. I remember Dad turning up and talking to her husband through the door, pleading to see me, and me refusing. Eventually, though, I agreed to talk to him and we went to a cafe. I remember Dad telling me how nothing mattered but that I come home.

That night Dad was so loving, so kind, reaching out to me, meeting me halfway, wanting me home.

But my lifestyle continued the same. I remember so many things: drinking after one guy practically forced me to have sex because I knew I'd been soiled and feeling like I couldn't go home; fleeing to the local park; looking a wreck and feeling a mess. I remember getting picked up by some guys in a night-club, going to a dark alley to smoke dope and get high, and having sex with them—then having to have an AIDS test (and the torment of waiting for the result).

Anyway I was feeling dead inside. I hated all the lying and I hated myself. A hunger was beginning to grow inside me, a hunger for something real, something to live for, something to die for. So it was that I was out one very wet evening, puffing on the end of a damp cigarette when I found myself heading for the Stream (a Saturday night youth service). I hadn't been for months, so this was bizarre. I can remember going in and sitting at the back, my hair hanging down around my face and concealing it.

It happened during the worship. It was as though the heavens opened. There was a bright beam of light and heat that was coming down from on high. It was as if there was no one else there except me and God. And he was saying, "You are mine." It was like real fire falling down from heaven, and my tears began to fall as I told God I was sorry for not loving him and praying that I could know him. I can remember saying yes to God that evening and saying yes to coming home. It was like God was saying, "It's all right, I'm going to meet all your needs and longings." As the tears fell and the repentance started, I felt so forgiven, so loved by God. He just kept saying, "You are mine" and I was replying, "I am yours." It was so freeing.

It was so wonderful.

Afterwards I told my parents I was sorry. I told them everything and watched them as they, too, cried. I learned that when they had prayed, things had happened—like the time when I'd run away. They'd prayed that they would find me and my friend had called them to tell them where I was.

God is so amazing. Those days of insecurity, of lack of confidence, of lack of hope, and lack of freedom seem so far away. I have just walked into his plan, and he has opened up door after door. I have been able to do a foundation course and am now doing a degree course. I met Peter and now we are married. We ran a group for fifteen- to eighteen year-olds in our home. It was great to meet the kids and be real with them. I was able to identify with them, and it's wonderful seeing them come to know the Lord and being able to pray with and talk to them about life.

My parents were fantastic through it all. They never stopped praying—and I know they never would have stopped, ever—not until I'd come home.

Chapter Eight

Pray They Meet the Father before They Meet the Elder Brother

All my adult life I have been captivated by the picture of the father in the parable running down the road towards his boy. When the old man reaches him, he throws himself on his son and begins kissing him. It is a wonderful image.

A friend illuminated it even more for me. He said, "It is a remarkable kiss—because of the pig-sty."

> "It is a remarkable kiss—because of the pig-sty."

I said, "What do you mean?"

My friend said, "The boy would have smelled of the pig sty, but the father didn't even mention it. He put a robe on top of those filthy clothes, a ring on the hand that was still stained with the swill, and shoes on the feet that had shared the mud with the animals. He could have said to the servants, 'Quick! Run a bath for my son!' and to the boy, 'As soon as you're cleaned up come into the house.' But this old man was wiser than that. He knew he must be patient; that even when the physical smell of his son's wanderings were gone, it would take time to leave it all behind. The prayers weren't all answered yet. The journey didn't end with the boy coming down the road. This was going to take time."

When our prodigals come home, we need to be patient with them. Don't let the first thing we say be, "I hope you've left that life behind forever." They may be bruised and scarred, hurting and confused. We can't expect them to have it all sorted out immediately. Some of them are not even sure of what needs to be sorted out. They don't necessarily want to put on a Sunday suit, rush to the prayer meeting, or say grace at the meal table, but they do know that, more than anywhere else on the face of the earth, they want to be home.

I think of one prodigal who said, "Be patient with me, Dad. I know there's lots wrong with me, but I do want to get my life turned around and get right with God again." In many ways it is rather like that other parable; they need a Samaritan who is willing to pour oil in their wounds, to love them, and give them rest.

Many of the prodigals I have met over the years have been people

> When our prodigals come home, we need to be patient with them.

> Sometimes they find the prospect of an immediate return to a local church just too daunting.

who have been Christians for years but have been bruised or broken in some way—perhaps by other Christians. Others are desperately ashamed of what they have done. Sometimes they find the prospect of an immediate return to a local church just too daunting.

For many years Dianne and I held a weekly meeting in our home; we called it "The Strugglers Group." All kinds of people came to it: some were prodigals, often people in mid-life who somehow had lost their way in the faith and wanted to take a step back towards God but were not quite sure how to; others came who had spent all their lives giving to those around them and now were burnt out; some had no faith at all. But whoever they were and whatever their story, all who came were looking for a safe haven for a while.

The atmosphere was very accepting. We often studied the Bible but we were just as likely to simply talk together. We prayed together every week but not with any expectation that everybody would join in, and nobody was ever asked to prepare "next week's topic." The truth is we often didn't have a "next week's topic"! We had few fixed agendas, and frankly nobody was ever sure whether that night we'd end up discussing "Why does God allow suffering?" or watch a film on television. And we tended not to get too excited if someone said something outrageous. After one woman had been coming for six months, she said, "On the first night I tried to shock you. But nobody took any notice."

> We tried to be honest and real with each other.

I suppose the key element is that we tried to love people just as they were and in whatever they were going through at that time. And we tried to be honest and *real* with each other. Over the years all kinds of people have asked to join the group, and I have often wondered why those who had vowed never to go into a church again came. Some said it felt like home, but I think it was more than that. I have a hunch that when people let their masks down, including the leaders, and genuinely reach out to God and to each other, then Jesus himself meets with them. Many who came not only rediscovered their own faith but then went on to help others in their journey. Some are now leading groups of their own.

Many prodigals have a clear view of where they have gone wrong.

Many prodigals have a clear view of where they have gone wrong, and people have not been reticent in pointing out where that was, but even as they tried to make their way home, they have sometimes found it hard to find encouragement. You may have a daughter who has been a prodigal. She has lived a selfish life, caring little for others. But one day she calls you and says, "Mom, I can't explain this, but I really believe that God is speaking to me. I know I'm not like all the others who go to your church but I feel I must spend some of my time working with disadvantaged kids in the evenings. There's still a lot I'm not sure about, but I've started praying in my room and asking God to forgive me, guide, and help me. I know there's a long way to go, and I don't really understand all that's going on, but I feel the need of God."

What that child needs is not a mother who says, "That's wonderful. Will you be in church next Sunday?" But rather, "Darling, this is what we have prayed for down the years. God has touched your life. We are so proud of what you are doing with those deprived kids. Let us know how we can go on praying for you."

Be patient with them. And be patient, too, in your waiting—

and yet look out for that action you can take which may hasten the return of your prodigals. It could be a letter, a visit, an apology, or perhaps just a phone call.

I remember speaking to a large group of church leaders; I was talking about how our kids can sometimes break our hearts. As I finished I said, "Some of you may want to call a son or daughter tonight and say, 'I know you have turned your back on everything we have ever believed, but this home is yours, the door is always open to you. Forgive us if we have ever given you the impression it was otherwise. We love you.'"

> "This home is yours, the door is always open."

A few days later I got a letter from one of those church leaders. He said, "We made the call that very night. We are beginning to rebuild a relationship we thought was gone forever."

And sometimes acceptance means we have to learn to love those that they love. Peter and Hilary were faced one day with the news that their son, Daniel, was

> "We made the call that very night."

moving in with his girlfriend. Afterwards they stayed up most of the night and talked about it. They felt sadder than they had felt for a long time, but in the early hours of the morning Hilary took her husband's hand and said, "Peter, all my life I have prayed that Dan would marry somebody who followed Christ, but that might not happen. Dan loves her, and I have decided that I *will* love her. And, if you can, I want you to join me in loving her too."

From that day on, every time Sally came to their house, she was hugged and welcomed. Her birthday was never missed, her opinion was both sought and respected. In short, Peter and Hilary loved her—at first as an act of the will. And then Sally's parents broke up rather suddenly, and a strange thing happened. She went straight to Hilary; she needed another woman. Hilary remembers holding her as she sobbed, and when Sally had gone, she turned to Peter and said, "I love that girl, really love her, and I believe she knows it."

> "I wasn't condoning it; I was shopping with her."

One day after church somebody said to Hilary, "I saw you out shopping with Sally the other day. How can you condone what she and Dan are doing?" Hilary thought for a moment and then said, "I wasn't condoning it; I was shopping with her. And in every shop and over every cup of coffee I was saying, 'I love you.' At first it was very hard—harder than you'll ever realize. But, you know, I am trying to be Jesus to that girl. And love is getting easier."

Sometimes our prodigals need time. God is not in a hurry. Listen to his Word:

> *But these things I plan won't happen right away. Slowly, steadily, surely, the time approaches when the vision will be fulfilled. If it seems slow, do not despair, for these things will surely come to pass. Just be patient! They will not be overdue a single day!*

> Habakkuk 2:3 *(Living Bible)*

Finally, remember the real reason why Jesus told this parable: the entrance of the elder brother is the dreadful sting in the tale and the awful condemnation of those who are so concerned with their own piety that they miss the breathless grace of God to the prodigals: those for whom the rules are more important than the forgiveness. He had overheard the religious leaders complaining that he was mixing with sinners and eating with them. These teachers of the law and Pharisees are like the elder brother with his whining, complaining, and careful guessing of the sins that his younger brother had committed: "He has squandered your money with prostitutes."

> Pray with all your hearts that they meet the father first and not the elder brother.

That spirit is still with us: if your prodigals do come home, pray with all your hearts that they meet the father first and not the elder brother. The elder brother will say, "Nice to see you back at church. But can I still smell alcohol on your breath? I hope you've broken up with that woman who was no good for you. Perhaps now you'll start taking your responsibilities here a little more seriously."

Oh, that elder brother! The one who did his sinning without ever leaving. The one who needed to "come home" every bit as much as his brother but who could never grasp what the heart of real love is—both to give and to receive it. The brother who never did get to a party—not even his own.

The elder brother simply couldn't understand the unconquerable nature of the father's love.

> The sheer wonder of his son's return had swept away the pain.

No catalog of rules broken, or pleas that it was all so unfair, can rob this father of joy. He is dancing with happiness: "Son, but we had to celebrate. Your brother was dead and is alive again, he was lost and is found." In a single moment, the sheer wonder of his son's return had swept away the pain of all the years of waiting, the gossip, the sleepless nights and the all-consuming fears.

It was over.

His boy was home.

Prayer

Oh Lord, I remember so clearly the first moment I held him. He was so tiny. I felt so proud and grateful to you for his safe birth. I prayed to you as I looked into his face, "Lord bless this child and keep him safe from all evil. Be with him every moment of his life and may he grow to love and serve you."

He's grown to be a good and loving son. I still feel so proud and grateful to you for him. He hasn't been to church much for a long time. Does that mean you're no longer with him? That he's never really loved you? That he'll never serve you?

Lord, protect me from doubt and lack of faith. I will repeat the prayer I said on the day he was born every day of my life.

Reflection

For God is able to "... carry out His purpose and do superabundantly, far over and above all that we dare ask or think—infinitely beyond our highest prayers, desires, thoughts, hopes or dreams."

Ephesians 3:20 (Amplified Bible)

Confirm, O Lord, that word of thine
That heavenly word of certainty,
Thou gavest it; I made it mine,
Believed to see.

And yet I see not; he for whom
That good word came in thy great love,
Is wandering still, and there is room
For fear to move.

O God of Hope, what though afar
From all desire that wanderer seems
Thy promise fails not; never are
Thy comforts dreams.

- Amy Carmichael

Carol's Prayer

I was thinking today of the time when my sister and I shared a bed as little girls. It was the bed where our mother sat with us to read Bible stories and where we said our prayers. The bed where some nights we kicked each other and where sometimes we cried in some shared childish grief, or laughed together till Dad came to the bottom of the stairs and told us to go to sleep. The bed where we talked about you, Lord. Where we wondered and questioned and grew to love you.

And then came the day when the bed was taken from our room, and two brand new ones replaced it. It wasn't too long after when I felt the first shock of awareness that it wasn't our faith anymore, it was my faith. Suddenly we were different from each other as never before. The core of my being, the thing most precious to me, my knowledge that you loved me, was something she denied, something she said she'd "outgrown."

We are so close. So much has happened—terrible times and wonderful times—and mostly we've been through them together. But it's not enough, Lord.

I want her back, Lord. I want it so much. I want her to know what it's like to be loved by you and to be forgiven. I want her to be safe, healed, made whole. I want her to love you.

It hurts. I'm angry and frustrated and guilty, and it's scary that she still seems such a long way off. It's hard to keep praying with faith, Lord.

Be with her, Lord. She's my sister. Bring her home soon.

Chapter Nine

Praying Home the Prodigals

To be involved in Bringing Home the Prodigals events through-out the world has been one of the greatest privileges of my life. Whether it has been in Europe, Asia, North America, or Australia, we have sought to capture the spirit of that day in 1998 when God first laid that message on my heart. The event is filled with worship, prayer, and teaching on prodigals, but everything moves towards the moment when people bring the names of those they love to God. Hundreds, sometimes thousands of people, write the names of their prodigals on a small card and bring it to the foot of the cross for prayer. We stand and pray for those we have named (using the prayer you will find at the end of the book), and then the stewards collect the baskets of names and take them to the exits. As people leave, they are asked to take a card from the basket and to pray for someone else's prodigal. If all the cards are not taken, we carry them with us to the next venue, which is often in a different town or even country. So it is that the Christians of America may pray for the prodigals of New Zealand; the Christians of Costa Rica pray for the prodigals of the United Kingdom, and the Christians of Australia pray for the prodigals of Malaysia.

People bring the names of those they love to God.

These events seem to me to be truly incredible, filled with such a high level of faith, hope, and what I can only describe as a touch of God. I have often considered why this is so, and I believe that much of it is to do with the attitude of the people who come. When those who have cried for prodigals—especially the parents of prodigals—come to pray, they often have a wonderful advantage: *they are humble.* These men and women have hearts that have been broken; they have learned that no person, book, or event is going to bring the answer to their prayers: they are totally dependent on God.

I believe that God wants us and *likes* us to feel our need of him, and when we are thrown completely on his grace because there is nowhere else to go, he hears our prayers. I cannot promise you that your prayers will be answered in the way that you want, but I do know that when we feel that God is our only hope, we are at the best place we can be.

If my people . . . will humble themselves and pray . . .
then will I hear from heaven.

2 Chronicles 7:14

It is significant that we lay the names of our prodigals at the foot of the cross. The cross of Christ is the greatest mystery in the world. It is a place of apparent defeat and yet unassailable victory; it is a place of tears and yet has in it the seeds of unbridled joy. The cross of Christ reminds us that the darkness of Good Friday gives way to the joy of Easter Sunday.

And there is no better place to bring your prodigal than to the cross. As we come with humble hearts to pray, we acknowledge that we have no answers, only painful memories, and little faith, and yet we commit those we love to Christ

> We lay the names of our prodigals at the foot of the cross.

and ask that by his grace he will bring them home.

Normally, two months before we go to a town or city with the Bringing Home the Prodigals event, I will invite the local church leaders to a seminar about it and ask them to encourage their members to attend. I had just finished one of these leaders' meetings when a young man came up to me. He told me that this was his first day as a church worker; he had just started in youth ministry. I congratulated him, and then he said, "My mother asked me to say hello." I asked him if I knew his mother and he smiled: "No. But four years ago, when I was breaking her heart, she came to a Bringing Home the Prodigals evening and laid my name at the foot of the cross."

When we returned to that city with the main event two months later, I told the audience about that conversation. During the interval

> "I am the mother whose heart was broken."

as I was making my way down an aisle, I felt someone tugging my jacket. I turned and a woman looked up at me from her seat and said, "I'm the mother." I will never forget that look. It was as if she was saying to me, "I am the mother whose heart was broken; I am the mother who at times felt that God wasn't listening to my cries;

I am the mother who almost despaired; I am the mother who kept on praying. I am the mother who never gave up."

But it isn't just in large venues that we see God at work. I will never forget being asked to speak to sixty or so people who were high level leaders in one of the main denominations. I shared my heart about the prodigals and told them of the incredible sight of seeing thousands of people lay the names of their prodigals at the foot of the cross. I spoke for only thirty minutes or so, and when I finished the chairman thanked me briefly and closed in prayer. The meeting was over, and I took my seat in the front row. Then someone shouted, "Does anyone have a cross? Why don't we see if there are some who have a prodigal on their hearts and would like to bring his or her name to God?" Somebody found a small cross and put it on a table at the front. We bowed our heads in prayer.

The table was full of names . . . behind me was filled with people waiting to get to the cross.

After a short while I looked up, but there were no names at the cross. I lowered my head. Suddenly a man started to cry. The cry turned into wailing, and when, after a few minutes, I next opened my eyes, I saw that the little table was full of names and the aisle behind me was filled with people waiting to get to the cross.

That experience showed me clearly that the heart of Bringing Home the Prodigals can be captured not only in vast auditoriums but among just a few—perhaps even in our home or church. It may be that all across the land, small groups will meet to pray for their precious ones.

Do not be afraid, for I am with you; I will bring your children from the east and gather you from the west. I will say to the north, "Give them up!" and to the south, "Do not hold them back." Bring my sons from afar and my daughters from the ends of the earth.

Isaiah 43:5

It is true that the parable we have considered together concerns a parent and child, but your prodigal may be a brother or sister, a husband, wife, friend, or even, in a strange reversal of the parable, a mother or father. But whoever they are, and wherever they are, remember that God loves your prodigals even more than you do.

Never stop praying, don't ever give up.

And always leave a light on.

Remember that God loves your prodigals even more than you do.

Prayer

Lord, only you know where our prodigals are—not just the physical place but in their hearts, their minds, their spirits. None of us can hide from you, and who is lost that you cannot find?

We pray for them. Lord, bring them home—not just to us, not even first to us, but to you. Forgive us if as parents, friends, or churches, we have made it easier for them to leave or harder to come back.

Wherever they are and whatever they are doing, touch their lives. And when they come home give us the spirit of the father and not the elder brother.

And, Lord, there are some of us who to the outside world seem never to have left the father's house, but we ourselves know how far we have wandered. Bring us back also.

And when they come back—those who have gone far away and those who have wandered near—then teach us all that sometimes in your kingdom it's not another meeting we need, but a party.